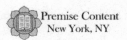

Premise Content
New York, NY

Sleep Journal

(8 Weeks of Tracking Your Sleep Patterns)

Helpful Tips

Sleep in a dark room (the darker the better.)

Sleep in a cool room (60 – 72 degrees.)

Make your sleep environment a comfortable space.

Make your bedroom as quiet as possible.

Sleep in something comfortable or in nothing at all.

Take time to relax and de-stress before you get into bed.

Create healthy habits by waking up and going to sleep at the same time each day and evening.

Avoid caffeine, nicotine, alcohol and heavy meals for 3-4 hours before sleep.

Get some exercise and sunlight during the day.

Remove electronics, cell phones and computers from your bedroom.

Before you sleep, think of three things you feel grateful to have in your life.

What hath night to do with sleep?

--John Milton, Paradise Lost

Day: _____ Date: _____

What time did I get into bed last night? _____

What time did I try to fall sleep? _____

What did I do in the time between getting into bed and trying to fall sleep? _____

How long did it take me to fall asleep? _____

How many times did I wake during the night? _____

What woke me? (What emotional, physical, environmental or other factors affected my sleep.)

_____
_____

Was I able to fall back asleep easily? If not, what did I do? Did I stay in bed or get out of bed?_____
_____

What did I do in the 1-2 hours before getting into bed?
_____
_____
_____
_____

What did I eat in the 2-3 hours before getting into bed?
_____
_____
_____
_____

Did I nap during the day? Yes / No
If so, for how long?_____

The quality of my sleep last night was:
Poor   1   2   3   4   5   6   7   8   9   10   Excellent

What time did I wake up in the morning? _____

What time did I get out of bed? _____

How rested did I feel in the morning?
Not rested at all   1   2   3   4   5   6   7   8   9   10   Very well rested

Did I have caffeine/nicotine/alcohol during the day? Y/N
What time(s)? _____
_____

What was my level of activity during the day?
Sedentary   Light   Moderate   Active   Extremely Active

Notes:
_____
_____
_____
_____
_____
_____
_____
_____
_____
_____
_____
_____

Day: _____ Date: _____

What time did I get into bed last night? _____

What time did I try to fall sleep? _____

What did I do in the time between getting into bed and trying to fall sleep? _____

How long did it take me to fall asleep? _____

How many times did I wake during the night? _____

What woke me? (What emotional, physical, environmental or other factors affected my sleep.)

_____

_____

Was I able to fall back asleep easily? If not, what did I do? Did I stay in bed or get out of bed?_____

_____

What did I do in the 1-2 hours before getting into bed?

_____

_____

_____

_____

What did I eat in the 2-3 hours before getting into bed?

_____

_____

_____

_____

Did I nap during the day? Yes / No
If so, for how long?_____

The quality of my sleep last night was:
Poor   1   2   3   4   5   6   7   8   9   10   Excellent

What time did I wake up in the morning? _____

What time did I get out of bed? _____

How rested did I feel in the morning?
Not rested at all   1   2   3   4   5   6   7   8   9   10   Very well rested

Did I have caffeine/nicotine/alcohol during the day? Y/N
What time(s)? _____
_____

What was my level of activity during the day?
Sedentary   Light   Moderate   Active   Extremely Active

Notes:
_____
_____
_____
_____
_____
_____
_____
_____
_____
_____
_____
_____

Day: _____ Date: _____

What time did I get into bed last night? _____

What time did I try to fall sleep? _____

What did I do in the time between getting into bed and trying to fall sleep? _____

How long did it take me to fall asleep? _____

How many times did I wake during the night? _____

What woke me? (What emotional, physical, environmental or other factors affected my sleep.)

_____

_____

Was I able to fall back asleep easily? If not, what did I do? Did I stay in bed or get out of bed?_____

_____

What did I do in the 1-2 hours before getting into bed?

_____

_____

_____

_____

What did I eat in the 2-3 hours before getting into bed?

_____

_____

_____

_____

Did I nap during the day? Yes / No
If so, for how long?_____

The quality of my sleep last night was:
Poor   1   2   3   4   5   6   7   8   9   10   Excellent

What time did I wake up in the morning? _____

What time did I get out of bed? _____

How rested did I feel in the morning?
Not rested at all   1   2   3   4   5   6   7   8   9   10   Very well rested

Did I have caffeine/nicotine/alcohol during the day? Y/N
What time(s)? _____
_____

What was my level of activity during the day?
Sedentary   Light   Moderate   Active   Extremely Active

Notes:
_____
_____
_____
_____
_____
_____
_____
_____
_____
_____
_____
_____

Day: _____   Date: _____

What time did I get into bed last night? _____

What time did I try to fall sleep? _____

What did I do in the time between getting into bed and trying to fall sleep? _____

How long did it take me to fall asleep? _____

How many times did I wake during the night? _____

What woke me? (What emotional, physical, environmental or other factors affected my sleep.)
_____
_____

Was I able to fall back asleep easily? If not, what did I do? Did I stay in bed or get out of bed?_____
_____

What did I do in the 1-2 hours before getting into bed?
_____
_____
_____
_____

What did I eat in the 2-3 hours before getting into bed?
_____
_____
_____
_____

Did I nap during the day? Yes / No
If so, for how long?_____

The quality of my sleep last night was:
Poor   1   2   3   4   5   6   7   8   9   10   Excellent

What time did I wake up in the morning?   _____

What time did I get out of bed?   _____

How rested did I feel in the morning?
Not rested at all   1   2   3   4   5   6   7   8   9   10   Very well rested

Did I have caffeine/nicotine/alcohol during the day? Y/N
What time(s)? _____
_____

What was my level of activity during the day?
Sedentary   Light   Moderate   Active   Extremely Active

Notes:
_____
_____
_____
_____
_____
_____
_____
_____
_____
_____
_____

Day: _____ Date: _____

What time did I get into bed last night? _____

What time did I try to fall sleep? _____

What did I do in the time between getting into bed and trying to fall sleep? _____

How long did it take me to fall asleep? _____

How many times did I wake during the night? _____

What woke me? (What emotional, physical, environmental or other factors affected my sleep.)
_____
_____

Was I able to fall back asleep easily? If not, what did I do? Did I stay in bed or get out of bed?_____
_____

What did I do in the 1-2 hours before getting into bed?
_____
_____
_____
_____

What did I eat in the 2-3 hours before getting into bed?
_____
_____
_____
_____

Did I nap during the day? Yes / No
If so, for how long?_____

The quality of my sleep last night was:
Poor   1   2   3   4   5   6   7   8   9   10   Excellent

What time did I wake up in the morning? _____

What time did I get out of bed? _____

How rested did I feel in the morning?
Not rested at all   1   2   3   4   5   6   7   8   9   10   Very well rested

Did I have caffeine/nicotine/alcohol during the day? Y/N
What time(s)? _____
_____

What was my level of activity during the day?
Sedentary   Light   Moderate   Active   Extremely Active

Notes:
_____
_____
_____
_____
_____
_____
_____
_____
_____
_____
_____
_____
_____

Day: _____ Date: _____

What time did I get into bed last night? _____

What time did I try to fall sleep? _____

What did I do in the time between getting into bed and trying to fall sleep? _____

How long did it take me to fall asleep? _____

How many times did I wake during the night? _____

What woke me? (What emotional, physical, environmental or other factors affected my sleep.)
_____
_____

Was I able to fall back asleep easily? If not, what did I do? Did I stay in bed or get out of bed?_____
_____

What did I do in the 1-2 hours before getting into bed?
_____
_____
_____
_____

What did I eat in the 2-3 hours before getting into bed?
_____
_____
_____
_____

Did I nap during the day? Yes / No
If so, for how long?_____

The quality of my sleep last night was:
Poor   1   2   3   4   5   6   7   8   9   10   Excellent

What time did I wake up in the morning? _____

What time did I get out of bed? _____

How rested did I feel in the morning?
Not rested at all   1   2   3   4   5   6   7   8   9   10   Very well rested

Did I have caffeine/nicotine/alcohol during the day? Y/N
What time(s)? _____
_____

What was my level of activity during the day?
Sedentary   Light   Moderate   Active   Extremely Active

Notes:
_____
_____
_____
_____
_____
_____
_____
_____
_____
_____
_____
_____

Day: _____ Date: _____

What time did I get into bed last night? _____

What time did I try to fall sleep? _____

What did I do in the time between getting into bed and trying to
fall sleep? _____

How long did it take me to fall asleep? _____

How many times did I wake during the night? _____

What woke me? (What emotional, physical, environmental or
other factors affected my sleep.)

_____
_____

Was I able to fall back asleep easily? If not, what did I do? Did I
stay in bed or get out of bed?_____
_____

What did I do in the 1-2 hours before getting into bed?

_____
_____
_____
_____

What did I eat in the 2-3 hours before getting into bed?

_____
_____
_____
_____

Did I nap during the day? Yes / No
If so, for how long?_____

The quality of my sleep last night was:
Poor   1   2   3   4   5   6   7   8   9   10   Excellent

What time did I wake up in the morning? _____

What time did I get out of bed? _____

How rested did I feel in the morning?
Not rested at all   1   2   3   4   5   6   7   8   9   10   Very well rested

Did I have caffeine/nicotine/alcohol during the day? Y/N
What time(s)? _____
_____

What was my level of activity during the day?
Sedentary   Light   Moderate   Active   Extremely Active

Notes:
_____
_____
_____
_____
_____
_____
_____
_____
_____
_____
_____
_____

Week-at-a-Glance

To track information in a week-at-a-glance, fill in the chart below. This will help you keep track of your basic sleep patterns.

Day of the Week	Day 1	Day 2	Day 3	Day 4	Day 5	Day 6	Day 7
What time did I get into bed?							
What time did I go to sleep?							
Total hours sleep							
Quality of Sleep (1-10)							
What time did I wake up?							
What time did I get out of bed?							
How rested did I feel? (1-10)							

Finish each day before you begin the next, and interpose a solid wall of sleep between the two.

--Ralph Waldo Emerson

Day: _____   Date: _____

What time did I get into bed last night? _____

What time did I try to fall sleep? _____

What did I do in the time between getting into bed and trying to fall sleep? _____

How long did it take me to fall asleep? _____

How many times did I wake during the night? _____

What woke me? (What emotional, physical, environmental or other factors affected my sleep.)

_____
_____

Was I able to fall back asleep easily? If not, what did I do? Did I stay in bed or get out of bed?_____
_____

What did I do in the 1-2 hours before getting into bed?

_____
_____
_____
_____

What did I eat in the 2-3 hours before getting into bed?

_____
_____
_____
_____

Did I nap during the day? Yes / No
If so, for how long?_____

The quality of my sleep last night was:
Poor   1   2   3   4   5   6   7   8   9   10   Excellent

What time did I wake up in the morning? _____

What time did I get out of bed? _____

How rested did I feel in the morning?
Not rested at all   1   2   3   4   5   6   7   8   9   10   Very well rested

Did I have caffeine/nicotine/alcohol during the day? Y/N
What time(s)? _____
_____

What was my level of activity during the day?
Sedentary   Light   Moderate   Active   Extremely Active

Notes:
_____
_____
_____
_____
_____
_____
_____
_____
_____
_____
_____
_____

Day: _____ Date: _____

What time did I get into bed last night? _____

What time did I try to fall sleep? _____

What did I do in the time between getting into bed and trying to fall sleep? _____

How long did it take me to fall asleep? _____

How many times did I wake during the night? _____

What woke me? (What emotional, physical, environmental or other factors affected my sleep.)

_____

_____

Was I able to fall back asleep easily? If not, what did I do? Did I stay in bed or get out of bed?_____

_____

What did I do in the 1-2 hours before getting into bed?

_____

_____

_____

_____

What did I eat in the 2-3 hours before getting into bed?

_____

_____

_____

_____

Did I nap during the day? Yes / No
If so, for how long?_____

The quality of my sleep last night was:
Poor   1   2   3   4   5   6   7   8   9   10   Excellent

What time did I wake up in the morning? _____

What time did I get out of bed? _____

How rested did I feel in the morning?
Not rested at all   1   2   3   4   5   6   7   8   9   10   Very well rested

Did I have caffeine/nicotine/alcohol during the day? Y/N
What time(s)? _____
_____

What was my level of activity during the day?
Sedentary   Light   Moderate   Active   Extremely Active

Notes:
_____
_____
_____
_____
_____
_____
_____
_____
_____
_____
_____
_____

Day: _____ Date: _____

What time did I get into bed last night? _____

What time did I try to fall sleep? _____

What did I do in the time between getting into bed and trying to fall sleep? _____

How long did it take me to fall asleep? _____

How many times did I wake during the night? _____

What woke me? (What emotional, physical, environmental or other factors affected my sleep.)

_____

_____

Was I able to fall back asleep easily? If not, what did I do? Did I stay in bed or get out of bed?_____

_____

What did I do in the 1-2 hours before getting into bed?

_____

_____

_____

_____

What did I eat in the 2-3 hours before getting into bed?

_____

_____

_____

_____

Did I nap during the day? Yes / No
If so, for how long?_____

The quality of my sleep last night was:
Poor   1   2   3   4   5   6   7   8   9   10   Excellent

What time did I wake up in the morning? _____

What time did I get out of bed? _____

How rested did I feel in the morning?
Not rested at all   1   2   3   4   5   6   7   8   9   10   Very well rested

Did I have caffeine/nicotine/alcohol during the day? Y/N
What time(s)? _____
_____

What was my level of activity during the day?
Sedentary   Light   Moderate   Active   Extremely Active

Notes:
_____
_____
_____
_____
_____
_____
_____
_____
_____
_____
_____
_____

Day: _____ Date: _____

What time did I get into bed last night? _____

What time did I try to fall sleep? _____

What did I do in the time between getting into bed and trying to fall sleep? _____

How long did it take me to fall asleep? _____

How many times did I wake during the night? _____

What woke me? (What emotional, physical, environmental or other factors affected my sleep.)
_____
_____

Was I able to fall back asleep easily? If not, what did I do? Did I stay in bed or get out of bed?_____
_____

What did I do in the 1-2 hours before getting into bed?
_____
_____
_____
_____

What did I eat in the 2-3 hours before getting into bed?
_____
_____
_____
_____

Did I nap during the day? Yes / No
If so, for how long?_____

The quality of my sleep last night was:
Poor   1   2   3   4   5   6   7   8   9   10   Excellent

What time did I wake up in the morning? _____

What time did I get out of bed? _____

How rested did I feel in the morning?
Not rested at all   1   2   3   4   5   6   7   8   9   10   Very well rested

Did I have caffeine/nicotine/alcohol during the day? Y/N
What time(s)? _____
_____

What was my level of activity during the day?
Sedentary   Light   Moderate   Active   Extremely Active

Notes:
_____
_____
_____
_____
_____
_____
_____
_____
_____
_____
_____
_____
_____
_____

Day: _____ Date: _____

What time did I get into bed last night? _____

What time did I try to fall sleep? _____

What did I do in the time between getting into bed and trying to fall sleep? _____

How long did it take me to fall asleep? _____

How many times did I wake during the night? _____

What woke me? (What emotional, physical, environmental or other factors affected my sleep.)

_____

_____

Was I able to fall back asleep easily? If not, what did I do? Did I stay in bed or get out of bed?_____

_____

What did I do in the 1-2 hours before getting into bed?

_____

_____

_____

_____

What did I eat in the 2-3 hours before getting into bed?

_____

_____

_____

_____

Did I nap during the day? Yes / No
If so, for how long?_____

The quality of my sleep last night was:
Poor   1   2   3   4   5   6   7   8   9   10   Excellent

What time did I wake up in the morning? _____

What time did I get out of bed? _____

How rested did I feel in the morning?
Not rested at all   1   2   3   4   5   6   7   8   9   10   Very well rested

Did I have caffeine/nicotine/alcohol during the day? Y/N
What time(s)? _____
_____

What was my level of activity during the day?
Sedentary   Light   Moderate   Active   Extremely Active

Notes:
_____
_____
_____
_____
_____
_____
_____
_____
_____
_____
_____
_____
_____

Day: _____ Date: _____

What time did I get into bed last night? _____

What time did I try to fall sleep? _____

What did I do in the time between getting into bed and trying to
fall sleep? _____

How long did it take me to fall asleep? _____

How many times did I wake during the night? _____

What woke me? (What emotional, physical, environmental or
other factors affected my sleep.)
_____
_____

Was I able to fall back asleep easily? If not, what did I do? Did I
stay in bed or get out of bed?_____
_____

What did I do in the 1-2 hours before getting into bed?
_____
_____
_____
_____

What did I eat in the 2-3 hours before getting into bed?
_____
_____
_____
_____

Did I nap during the day? Yes / No
If so, for how long?_____

The quality of my sleep last night was:
Poor   1   2   3   4   5   6   7   8   9   10   Excellent

What time did I wake up in the morning? _____

What time did I get out of bed? _____

How rested did I feel in the morning?
Not rested at all   1   2   3   4   5   6   7   8   9   10   Very well rested

Did I have caffeine/nicotine/alcohol during the day? Y/N
What time(s)? _____
_____

What was my level of activity during the day?
Sedentary   Light   Moderate   Active   Extremely Active

Notes:
_____
_____
_____
_____
_____
_____
_____
_____
_____
_____
_____
_____
_____

Day: _____ Date: _____

What time did I get into bed last night? _____

What time did I try to fall sleep? _____

What did I do in the time between getting into bed and trying to fall sleep? _____

How long did it take me to fall asleep? _____

How many times did I wake during the night? _____

What woke me? (What emotional, physical, environmental or other factors affected my sleep.)

_____

_____

Was I able to fall back asleep easily? If not, what did I do? Did I stay in bed or get out of bed?_____

_____

What did I do in the 1-2 hours before getting into bed?

_____

_____

_____

_____

What did I eat in the 2-3 hours before getting into bed?

_____

_____

_____

_____

Did I nap during the day? Yes / No
If so, for how long?_____

The quality of my sleep last night was:
Poor   1   2   3   4   5   6   7   8   9   10   Excellent

What time did I wake up in the morning? _____

What time did I get out of bed? _____

How rested did I feel in the morning?
Not rested at all   1   2   3   4   5   6   7   8   9   10   Very well rested

Did I have caffeine/nicotine/alcohol during the day? Y/N
What time(s)? _____
_____

What was my level of activity during the day?
Sedentary   Light   Moderate   Active   Extremely Active

Notes:
_____
_____
_____
_____
_____
_____
_____
_____
_____
_____
_____
_____

Week-at-a-Glance

To track information in a week-at-a-glance, fill in the chart below. This will help you keep track of your basic sleep patterns.

Day of the Week	Day 1	Day 2	Day 3	Day 4	Day 5	Day 6	Day 7
What time did I get into bed?							
What time did I go to sleep?							
Total hours sleep							
Quality of Sleep (1-10)							
What time did I wake up?							
What time did I get out of bed?							
How rested did I feel? (1-10)							

Fatigue is the best pillow.

--Benjamin Franklin

Day: _____ Date: _____

What time did I get into bed last night? _____

What time did I try to fall sleep? _____

What did I do in the time between getting into bed and trying to fall sleep? _____

How long did it take me to fall asleep? _____

How many times did I wake during the night? _____

What woke me? (What emotional, physical, environmental or other factors affected my sleep.)
_____
_____

Was I able to fall back asleep easily? If not, what did I do? Did I stay in bed or get out of bed?_____
_____

What did I do in the 1-2 hours before getting into bed?
_____
_____
_____
_____

What did I eat in the 2-3 hours before getting into bed?
_____
_____
_____
_____

Did I nap during the day? Yes / No
If so, for how long?_____

The quality of my sleep last night was:
Poor   1   2   3   4   5   6   7   8   9   10   Excellent

What time did I wake up in the morning? _____

What time did I get out of bed? _____

How rested did I feel in the morning?
Not rested at all   1   2   3   4   5   6   7   8   9   10   Very well rested

Did I have caffeine/nicotine/alcohol during the day? Y/N
What time(s)? _____
_____

What was my level of activity during the day?
Sedentary   Light   Moderate   Active   Extremely Active

Notes:
_____
_____
_____
_____
_____
_____
_____
_____
_____
_____
_____
_____

Day: _____ Date: _____

What time did I get into bed last night? _____

What time did I try to fall sleep? _____

What did I do in the time between getting into bed and trying to fall sleep? _____

How long did it take me to fall asleep? _____

How many times did I wake during the night? _____

What woke me? (What emotional, physical, environmental or other factors affected my sleep.)

_____

_____

Was I able to fall back asleep easily? If not, what did I do? Did I stay in bed or get out of bed?_____

_____

What did I do in the 1-2 hours before getting into bed?

_____

_____

_____

_____

What did I eat in the 2-3 hours before getting into bed?

_____

_____

_____

_____

Did I nap during the day? Yes / No
If so, for how long?_____

The quality of my sleep last night was:
Poor   1   2   3   4   5   6   7   8   9   10   Excellent

What time did I wake up in the morning? _____

What time did I get out of bed? _____

How rested did I feel in the morning?
Not rested at all   1   2   3   4   5   6   7   8   9   10   Very well rested

Did I have caffeine/nicotine/alcohol during the day? Y/N
What time(s)? _____
_____

What was my level of activity during the day?
Sedentary   Light   Moderate   Active   Extremely Active

Notes:
_____
_____
_____
_____
_____
_____
_____
_____
_____
_____
_____
_____
_____

Day: _____ Date: _____

What time did I get into bed last night? _____

What time did I try to fall sleep? _____

What did I do in the time between getting into bed and trying to fall sleep? _____

How long did it take me to fall asleep? _____

How many times did I wake during the night? _____

What woke me? (What emotional, physical, environmental or other factors affected my sleep.)
_____
_____

Was I able to fall back asleep easily? If not, what did I do? Did I stay in bed or get out of bed?_____
_____

What did I do in the 1-2 hours before getting into bed?
_____
_____
_____
_____

What did I eat in the 2-3 hours before getting into bed?
_____
_____
_____
_____

Did I nap during the day? Yes / No
If so, for how long?_____

The quality of my sleep last night was:
Poor   1   2   3   4   5   6   7   8   9   10   Excellent

What time did I wake up in the morning? _____

What time did I get out of bed? _____

How rested did I feel in the morning?
Not rested at all   1   2   3   4   5   6   7   8   9   10   Very well rested

Did I have caffeine/nicotine/alcohol during the day? Y/N
What time(s)? _____
_____

What was my level of activity during the day?
Sedentary   Light   Moderate   Active   Extremely Active

Notes:
_____
_____
_____
_____
_____
_____
_____
_____
_____
_____
_____
_____
_____

Day: _____ Date: _____

What time did I get into bed last night? _____

What time did I try to fall sleep? _____

What did I do in the time between getting into bed and trying to fall sleep? _____

How long did it take me to fall asleep? _____

How many times did I wake during the night? _____

What woke me? (What emotional, physical, environmental or other factors affected my sleep.)

_____

_____

Was I able to fall back asleep easily? If not, what did I do? Did I stay in bed or get out of bed?_____

_____

What did I do in the 1-2 hours before getting into bed?

_____

_____

_____

_____

What did I eat in the 2-3 hours before getting into bed?

_____

_____

_____

_____

Did I nap during the day? Yes / No
If so, for how long?_____

The quality of my sleep last night was:
Poor   1   2   3   4   5   6   7   8   9   10   Excellent

What time did I wake up in the morning? _____

What time did I get out of bed? _____

How rested did I feel in the morning?
Not rested at all   1   2   3   4   5   6   7   8   9   10   Very well rested

Did I have caffeine/nicotine/alcohol during the day? Y/N
What time(s)? _____
_____

What was my level of activity during the day?
Sedentary   Light   Moderate   Active   Extremely Active

Notes:
_____
_____
_____
_____
_____
_____
_____
_____
_____
_____
_____
_____

Day: _____ Date: _____

What time did I get into bed last night? _____

What time did I try to fall sleep? _____

What did I do in the time between getting into bed and trying to fall sleep? _____

How long did it take me to fall asleep? _____

How many times did I wake during the night? _____

What woke me? (What emotional, physical, environmental or other factors affected my sleep.)

_____
_____

Was I able to fall back asleep easily? If not, what did I do? Did I stay in bed or get out of bed?_____
_____

What did I do in the 1-2 hours before getting into bed?

_____
_____
_____
_____

What did I eat in the 2-3 hours before getting into bed?

_____
_____
_____
_____

Did I nap during the day? Yes / No
If so, for how long?_____

The quality of my sleep last night was:
Poor   1   2   3   4   5   6   7   8   9   10   Excellent

What time did I wake up in the morning? _____

What time did I get out of bed? _____

How rested did I feel in the morning?
Not rested at all   1   2   3   4   5   6   7   8   9   10   Very well rested

Did I have caffeine/nicotine/alcohol during the day? Y/N
What time(s)? _____
_____

What was my level of activity during the day?
Sedentary   Light   Moderate   Active   Extremely Active

Notes:
_____
_____
_____
_____
_____
_____
_____
_____
_____
_____
_____

Day: _____   Date: _____

What time did I get into bed last night? _____

What time did I try to fall sleep? _____

What did I do in the time between getting into bed and trying to fall sleep? _____

How long did it take me to fall asleep? _____

How many times did I wake during the night? _____

What woke me? (What emotional, physical, environmental or other factors affected my sleep.)
_____
_____

Was I able to fall back asleep easily? If not, what did I do? Did I stay in bed or get out of bed?_____
_____

What did I do in the 1-2 hours before getting into bed?
_____
_____
_____
_____

What did I eat in the 2-3 hours before getting into bed?
_____
_____
_____
_____

Did I nap during the day? Yes / No
If so, for how long?_____

The quality of my sleep last night was:
Poor   1   2   3   4   5   6   7   8   9   10   Excellent

What time did I wake up in the morning? _____

What time did I get out of bed? _____

How rested did I feel in the morning?
Not rested at all   1   2   3   4   5   6   7   8   9   10   Very well rested

Did I have caffeine/nicotine/alcohol during the day? Y/N
What time(s)? _____
_____

What was my level of activity during the day?
Sedentary   Light   Moderate   Active   Extremely Active

Notes:
_____
_____
_____
_____
_____
_____
_____
_____
_____
_____
_____
_____
_____

Day: _____ Date: _____

What time did I get into bed last night? _____

What time did I try to fall sleep? _____

What did I do in the time between getting into bed and trying to fall sleep? _____

How long did it take me to fall asleep? _____

How many times did I wake during the night? _____

What woke me? (What emotional, physical, environmental or other factors affected my sleep.)
_____
_____

Was I able to fall back asleep easily? If not, what did I do? Did I stay in bed or get out of bed?_____
_____

What did I do in the 1-2 hours before getting into bed?
_____
_____
_____
_____

What did I eat in the 2-3 hours before getting into bed?
_____
_____
_____
_____

Did I nap during the day? Yes / No
If so, for how long?_____

The quality of my sleep last night was:
Poor   1   2   3   4   5   6   7   8   9   10   Excellent

What time did I wake up in the morning? _____

What time did I get out of bed? _____

How rested did I feel in the morning?
Not rested at all   1 2 3 4 5 6 7 8 9 10   Very well rested

Did I have caffeine/nicotine/alcohol during the day? Y/N
What time(s)? _____
_____

What was my level of activity during the day?
Sedentary   Light   Moderate   Active   Extremely Active

Notes:
_____
_____
_____
_____
_____
_____
_____
_____
_____
_____
_____
_____
_____

Week-at-a-Glance

To track information in a week-at-a-glance, fill in the chart below. This will help you keep track of your basic sleep patterns.

Day of the Week	Day 1	Day 2	Day 3	Day 4	Day 5	Day 6	Day 7
What time did I get into bed?							
What time did I go to sleep?							
Total hours sleep							
Quality of Sleep (1-10)							
What time did I wake up?							
What time did I get out of bed?							
How rested did I feel? (1-10)							

It appears that every man's insomnia is as different from his
neighbor's as are their daytime hopes and aspirations.

--F. Scott Fitzgerald

Day: _____ Date: _____

What time did I get into bed last night? _____

What time did I try to fall sleep? _____

What did I do in the time between getting into bed and trying to fall sleep? _____

How long did it take me to fall asleep? _____

How many times did I wake during the night? _____

What woke me? (What emotional, physical, environmental or other factors affected my sleep.)

_____
_____

Was I able to fall back asleep easily? If not, what did I do? Did I stay in bed or get out of bed?_____
_____

What did I do in the 1-2 hours before getting into bed?

_____
_____
_____
_____

What did I eat in the 2-3 hours before getting into bed?

_____
_____
_____
_____

Did I nap during the day? Yes / No
If so, for how long?_____

The quality of my sleep last night was:
Poor   1   2   3   4   5   6   7   8   9   10   Excellent

What time did I wake up in the morning? _____

What time did I get out of bed? _____

How rested did I feel in the morning?
Not rested at all   1   2   3   4   5   6   7   8   9   10   Very well rested

Did I have caffeine/nicotine/alcohol during the day? Y/N
What time(s)? _____
_____

What was my level of activity during the day?
Sedentary   Light   Moderate   Active   Extremely Active

Notes:
_____
_____
_____
_____
_____
_____
_____
_____
_____
_____
_____
_____

Day: _____ Date: _____

What time did I get into bed last night? _____

What time did I try to fall sleep? _____

What did I do in the time between getting into bed and trying to fall sleep? _____

How long did it take me to fall asleep? _____

How many times did I wake during the night? _____

What woke me? (What emotional, physical, environmental or other factors affected my sleep.)
_____
_____

Was I able to fall back asleep easily? If not, what did I do? Did I stay in bed or get out of bed?_____
_____

What did I do in the 1-2 hours before getting into bed?
_____
_____
_____
_____

What did I eat in the 2-3 hours before getting into bed?
_____
_____
_____
_____

Did I nap during the day? Yes / No

If so, for how long?_____

The quality of my sleep last night was:

Poor   1   2   3   4   5   6   7   8   9   10   Excellent

What time did I wake up in the morning? _____

What time did I get out of bed? _____

How rested did I feel in the morning?

Not rested at all   1   2   3   4   5   6   7   8   9   10   Very well rested

Did I have caffeine/nicotine/alcohol during the day? Y/N

What time(s)? _____
_____

What was my level of activity during the day?

Sedentary   Light   Moderate   Active   Extremely Active

Notes:

_____
_____
_____
_____
_____
_____
_____
_____
_____
_____
_____
_____
_____

Day: _____ Date: _____

What time did I get into bed last night? _____

What time did I try to fall sleep? _____

What did I do in the time between getting into bed and trying to fall sleep? _____

How long did it take me to fall asleep? _____

How many times did I wake during the night? _____

What woke me? (What emotional, physical, environmental or other factors affected my sleep.)
_____
_____

Was I able to fall back asleep easily? If not, what did I do? Did I stay in bed or get out of bed?_____
_____

What did I do in the 1-2 hours before getting into bed?
_____
_____
_____
_____

What did I eat in the 2-3 hours before getting into bed?
_____
_____
_____
_____

Did I nap during the day? Yes / No
If so, for how long?_____

The quality of my sleep last night was:
Poor   1   2   3   4   5   6   7   8   9   10   Excellent

What time did I wake up in the morning? _____

What time did I get out of bed? _____

How rested did I feel in the morning?
Not rested at all   1   2   3   4   5   6   7   8   9   10   Very well rested

Did I have caffeine/nicotine/alcohol during the day? Y/N
What time(s)? _____
_____

What was my level of activity during the day?
Sedentary   Light   Moderate   Active   Extremely Active

Notes:
_____
_____
_____
_____
_____
_____
_____
_____
_____
_____
_____
_____

Day: _____ Date: _____

What time did I get into bed last night? _____

What time did I try to fall sleep? _____

What did I do in the time between getting into bed and trying to fall sleep? _____

How long did it take me to fall asleep? _____

How many times did I wake during the night? _____

What woke me? (What emotional, physical, environmental or other factors affected my sleep.)

_____
_____

Was I able to fall back asleep easily? If not, what did I do? Did I stay in bed or get out of bed?_____
_____

What did I do in the 1-2 hours before getting into bed?

_____
_____
_____
_____

What did I eat in the 2-3 hours before getting into bed?

_____
_____
_____
_____

Did I nap during the day? Yes / No
If so, for how long?_____

The quality of my sleep last night was:
Poor   1   2   3   4   5   6   7   8   9   10   Excellent

What time did I wake up in the morning? _____

What time did I get out of bed? _____

How rested did I feel in the morning?
Not rested at all   1   2   3   4   5   6   7   8   9   10   Very well rested

Did I have caffeine/nicotine/alcohol during the day? Y/N
What time(s)? _____
_____

What was my level of activity during the day?
Sedentary   Light   Moderate   Active   Extremely Active

Notes:
_____
_____
_____
_____
_____
_____
_____
_____
_____
_____
_____
_____

Day: _____   Date: _____

What time did I get into bed last night? _____

What time did I try to fall sleep? _____

What did I do in the time between getting into bed and trying to fall sleep? _____

How long did it take me to fall asleep? _____

How many times did I wake during the night? _____

What woke me? (What emotional, physical, environmental or other factors affected my sleep.)
_____
_____

Was I able to fall back asleep easily? If not, what did I do? Did I stay in bed or get out of bed?_____
_____

What did I do in the 1-2 hours before getting into bed?
_____
_____
_____
_____

What did I eat in the 2-3 hours before getting into bed?
_____
_____
_____
_____

Did I nap during the day? Yes / No
If so, for how long?_____

The quality of my sleep last night was:
Poor   1   2   3   4   5   6   7   8   9   10   Excellent

What time did I wake up in the morning? _____

What time did I get out of bed? _____

How rested did I feel in the morning?
Not rested at all   1   2   3   4   5   6   7   8   9   10   Very well rested

Did I have caffeine/nicotine/alcohol during the day? Y/N
What time(s)? _____
_____

What was my level of activity during the day?
Sedentary   Light   Moderate   Active   Extremely Active

Notes:
_____
_____
_____
_____
_____
_____
_____
_____
_____
_____
_____
_____

Day: _____ Date: _____

What time did I get into bed last night? _____

What time did I try to fall sleep? _____

What did I do in the time between getting into bed and trying to
fall sleep? _____

How long did it take me to fall asleep? _____

How many times did I wake during the night? _____

What woke me? (What emotional, physical, environmental or
other factors affected my sleep.)
_____
_____

Was I able to fall back asleep easily? If not, what did I do? Did I
stay in bed or get out of bed?_____
_____

What did I do in the 1-2 hours before getting into bed?
_____
_____
_____
_____

What did I eat in the 2-3 hours before getting into bed?
_____
_____
_____
_____

Did I nap during the day? Yes / No
If so, for how long?_____

The quality of my sleep last night was:
Poor   1   2   3   4   5   6   7   8   9   10   Excellent

What time did I wake up in the morning? _____

What time did I get out of bed? _____

How rested did I feel in the morning?
Not rested at all   1   2   3   4   5   6   7   8   9   10   Very well rested

Did I have caffeine/nicotine/alcohol during the day? Y/N
What time(s)? _____
_____

What was my level of activity during the day?
Sedentary   Light   Moderate   Active   Extremely Active

Notes:
_____
_____
_____
_____
_____
_____
_____
_____
_____
_____
_____
_____
_____

Day: _____ Date: _____

What time did I get into bed last night? _____

What time did I try to fall sleep? _____

What did I do in the time between getting into bed and trying to fall sleep? _____

How long did it take me to fall asleep? _____

How many times did I wake during the night? _____

What woke me? (What emotional, physical, environmental or other factors affected my sleep.)

_____

_____

Was I able to fall back asleep easily? If not, what did I do? Did I stay in bed or get out of bed?_____

_____

What did I do in the 1-2 hours before getting into bed?

_____

_____

_____

_____

What did I eat in the 2-3 hours before getting into bed?

_____

_____

_____

_____

Did I nap during the day? Yes / No
If so, for how long?_____

The quality of my sleep last night was:
Poor   1   2   3   4   5   6   7   8   9   10   Excellent

What time did I wake up in the morning? _____

What time did I get out of bed? _____

How rested did I feel in the morning?
Not rested at all   1   2   3   4   5   6   7   8   9   10   Very well rested

Did I have caffeine/nicotine/alcohol during the day? Y/N
What time(s)? _____
_____

What was my level of activity during the day?
Sedentary   Light   Moderate   Active   Extremely Active

Notes:
_____
_____
_____
_____
_____
_____
_____
_____
_____
_____
_____
_____
_____

Week-at-a-Glance

To track information in a week-at-a-glance, fill in the chart below. This will help you keep track of your basic sleep patterns.

Day of the Week	Day 1	Day 2	Day 3	Day 4	Day 5	Day 6	Day 7
What time did I get into bed?							
What time did I go to sleep?							
Total hours sleep							
Quality of Sleep (1-10)							
What time did I wake up?							
What time did I get out of bed?							
How rested did I feel? (1-10)							

Sleep is the best meditation.

--Dalai Lama

Day: _____ Date: _____

What time did I get into bed last night? _____

What time did I try to fall sleep? _____

What did I do in the time between getting into bed and trying to fall sleep? _____

How long did it take me to fall asleep? _____

How many times did I wake during the night? _____

What woke me? (What emotional, physical, environmental or other factors affected my sleep.)
_____
_____

Was I able to fall back asleep easily? If not, what did I do? Did I stay in bed or get out of bed?_____
_____

What did I do in the 1-2 hours before getting into bed?
_____
_____
_____
_____

What did I eat in the 2-3 hours before getting into bed?
_____
_____
_____
_____

Did I nap during the day? Yes / No
 If so, for how long?_____

The quality of my sleep last night was:
Poor   1 2 3 4 5 6 7 8 9 10   Excellent

What time did I wake up in the morning? _____

What time did I get out of bed? _____

How rested did I feel in the morning?
Not rested at all 1 2 3 4 5 6 7 8 9 10 Very well rested

Did I have caffeine/nicotine/alcohol during the day? Y/N
What time(s)? _____
_____

What was my level of activity during the day?
Sedentary   Light   Moderate   Active   Extremely Active

Notes:
_____
_____
_____
_____
_____
_____
_____
_____
_____
_____
_____
_____

Day: _____ Date: _____

What time did I get into bed last night? _____

What time did I try to fall sleep? _____

What did I do in the time between getting into bed and trying to fall sleep? _____

How long did it take me to fall asleep? _____

How many times did I wake during the night? _____

What woke me? (What emotional, physical, environmental or other factors affected my sleep.)

_____

_____

Was I able to fall back asleep easily? If not, what did I do? Did I stay in bed or get out of bed?_____

_____

What did I do in the 1-2 hours before getting into bed?

_____

_____

_____

_____

What did I eat in the 2-3 hours before getting into bed?

_____

_____

_____

_____

Did I nap during the day? Yes / No

If so, for how long?_____

The quality of my sleep last night was:

Poor   1   2   3   4   5   6   7   8   9   10   Excellent

What time did I wake up in the morning? _____

What time did I get out of bed? _____

How rested did I feel in the morning?

Not rested at all   1   2   3   4   5   6   7   8   9   10   Very well rested

Did I have caffeine/nicotine/alcohol during the day? Y/N

What time(s)? _____
_____

What was my level of activity during the day?

Sedentary   Light   Moderate   Active   Extremely Active

Notes:
_____
_____
_____
_____
_____
_____
_____
_____
_____
_____
_____
_____

Day: _____   Date: _____

What time did I get into bed last night? _____

What time did I try to fall sleep? _____

What did I do in the time between getting into bed and trying to fall sleep? _____

How long did it take me to fall asleep? _____

How many times did I wake during the night? _____

What woke me? (What emotional, physical, environmental or other factors affected my sleep.)

_____

_____

Was I able to fall back asleep easily? If not, what did I do? Did I stay in bed or get out of bed?_____

_____

What did I do in the 1-2 hours before getting into bed?

_____

_____

_____

_____

What did I eat in the 2-3 hours before getting into bed?

_____

_____

_____

_____

Did I nap during the day? Yes / No
If so, for how long?_____

The quality of my sleep last night was:
Poor   1   2   3   4   5   6   7   8   9   10   Excellent

What time did I wake up in the morning? _____

What time did I get out of bed? _____

How rested did I feel in the morning?
Not rested at all   1   2   3   4   5   6   7   8   9   10   Very well rested

Did I have caffeine/nicotine/alcohol during the day? Y/N
What time(s)? _____
_____

What was my level of activity during the day?
Sedentary   Light   Moderate   Active   Extremely Active

Notes:
_____
_____
_____
_____
_____
_____
_____
_____
_____
_____
_____
_____

Day: _____   Date: _____

What time did I get into bed last night? _____

What time did I try to fall sleep? _____

What did I do in the time between getting into bed and trying to fall sleep? _____

How long did it take me to fall asleep? _____

How many times did I wake during the night? _____

What woke me? (What emotional, physical, environmental or other factors affected my sleep.)
_____
_____

Was I able to fall back asleep easily? If not, what did I do? Did I stay in bed or get out of bed?_____
_____

What did I do in the 1-2 hours before getting into bed?
_____
_____
_____
_____

What did I eat in the 2-3 hours before getting into bed?
_____
_____
_____
_____

Did I nap during the day? Yes / No
If so, for how long?_____

The quality of my sleep last night was:
Poor   1   2   3   4   5   6   7   8   9   10   Excellent

What time did I wake up in the morning? _____

What time did I get out of bed? _____

How rested did I feel in the morning?
Not rested at all   1   2   3   4   5   6   7   8   9   10   Very well rested

Did I have caffeine/nicotine/alcohol during the day? Y/N
What time(s)? _____
_____

What was my level of activity during the day?
Sedentary   Light   Moderate   Active   Extremely Active

Notes:
_____
_____
_____
_____
_____
_____
_____
_____
_____
_____
_____
_____
_____
_____

Day: _____ Date: _____

What time did I get into bed last night? _____

What time did I try to fall sleep? _____

What did I do in the time between getting into bed and trying to fall sleep? _____

How long did it take me to fall asleep? _____

How many times did I wake during the night? _____

What woke me? (What emotional, physical, environmental or other factors affected my sleep.)

_____

_____

Was I able to fall back asleep easily? If not, what did I do? Did I stay in bed or get out of bed?_____

_____

What did I do in the 1-2 hours before getting into bed?

_____

_____

_____

_____

What did I eat in the 2-3 hours before getting into bed?

_____

_____

_____

_____

Did I nap during the day? Yes / No
If so, for how long?_____

The quality of my sleep last night was:
Poor   1   2   3   4   5   6   7   8   9   10   Excellent

What time did I wake up in the morning? _____

What time did I get out of bed? _____

How rested did I feel in the morning?
Not rested at all   1   2   3   4   5   6   7   8   9   10   Very well rested

Did I have caffeine/nicotine/alcohol during the day? Y/N
What time(s)? _____
_____

What was my level of activity during the day?
Sedentary   Light   Moderate   Active   Extremely Active

Notes:
_____
_____
_____
_____
_____
_____
_____
_____
_____
_____
_____
_____
_____

Day: _____ Date: _____

What time did I get into bed last night? _____

What time did I try to fall sleep? _____

What did I do in the time between getting into bed and trying to fall sleep? _____

How long did it take me to fall asleep? _____

How many times did I wake during the night? _____

What woke me? (What emotional, physical, environmental or other factors affected my sleep.)
_____
_____

Was I able to fall back asleep easily? If not, what did I do? Did I stay in bed or get out of bed?_____
_____

What did I do in the 1-2 hours before getting into bed?
_____
_____
_____
_____

What did I eat in the 2-3 hours before getting into bed?
_____
_____
_____
_____

Did I nap during the day? Yes / No

If so, for how long?_____

The quality of my sleep last night was:

Poor   1   2   3   4   5   6   7   8   9   10   Excellent

What time did I wake up in the morning? _____

What time did I get out of bed? _____

How rested did I feel in the morning?

Not rested at all   1   2   3   4   5   6   7   8   9   10   Very well rested

Did I have caffeine/nicotine/alcohol during the day? Y/N

What time(s)? _____
_____

What was my level of activity during the day?

Sedentary   Light   Moderate   Active   Extremely Active

Notes:

_____
_____
_____
_____
_____
_____
_____
_____
_____
_____
_____
_____
_____

Day: _____ Date: _____

What time did I get into bed last night? _____

What time did I try to fall sleep? _____

What did I do in the time between getting into bed and trying to fall sleep? _____

How long did it take me to fall asleep? _____

How many times did I wake during the night? _____

What woke me? (What emotional, physical, environmental or other factors affected my sleep.)

_____

_____

Was I able to fall back asleep easily? If not, what did I do? Did I stay in bed or get out of bed?_____

_____

What did I do in the 1-2 hours before getting into bed?

_____

_____

_____

_____

What did I eat in the 2-3 hours before getting into bed?

_____

_____

_____

_____

Did I nap during the day? Yes / No
If so, for how long?_____

The quality of my sleep last night was:
Poor   1   2   3   4   5   6   7   8   9   10   Excellent

What time did I wake up in the morning? _____

What time did I get out of bed? _____

How rested did I feel in the morning?
Not rested at all   1   2   3   4   5   6   7   8   9   10   Very well rested

Did I have caffeine/nicotine/alcohol during the day? Y/N
What time(s)? _____
_____

What was my level of activity during the day?
Sedentary   Light   Moderate   Active   Extremely Active

Notes:
_____
_____
_____
_____
_____
_____
_____
_____
_____
_____
_____
_____

Week-at-a-Glance

To track information in a week-at-a-glance, fill in the chart below. This will help you keep track of your basic sleep patterns.

Day of the Week	Day 1	Day 2	Day 3	Day 4	Day 5	Day 6	Day 7
What time did I get into bed?							
What time did I go to sleep?							
Total hours sleep							
Quality of Sleep (1-10)							
What time did I wake up?							
What time did I get out of bed?							
How rested did I feel? (1-10)							

The last refuge of the insomniac is a sense of superiority to the sleeping world.

--Leonard Cohen

Day: _____ Date: _____

What time did I get into bed last night? _____

What time did I try to fall sleep? _____

What did I do in the time between getting into bed and trying to fall sleep? _____

How long did it take me to fall asleep? _____

How many times did I wake during the night? _____

What woke me? (What emotional, physical, environmental or other factors affected my sleep.)

_____

_____

Was I able to fall back asleep easily? If not, what did I do? Did I stay in bed or get out of bed?_____

_____

What did I do in the 1-2 hours before getting into bed?

_____

_____

_____

_____

What did I eat in the 2-3 hours before getting into bed?

_____

_____

_____

_____

Did I nap during the day? Yes / No
If so, for how long?_____

The quality of my sleep last night was:
Poor   1   2   3   4   5   6   7   8   9   10   Excellent

What time did I wake up in the morning? _____

What time did I get out of bed? _____

How rested did I feel in the morning?
Not rested at all   1   2   3   4   5   6   7   8   9   10   Very well rested

Did I have caffeine/nicotine/alcohol during the day? Y/N
What time(s)? _____
_____

What was my level of activity during the day?
Sedentary   Light   Moderate   Active   Extremely Active

Notes:
_____
_____
_____
_____
_____
_____
_____
_____
_____
_____
_____
_____

Day: _____ Date: _____

What time did I get into bed last night? _____

What time did I try to fall sleep? _____

What did I do in the time between getting into bed and trying to fall sleep? _____

How long did it take me to fall asleep? _____

How many times did I wake during the night? _____

What woke me? (What emotional, physical, environmental or other factors affected my sleep.)
_____
_____

Was I able to fall back asleep easily? If not, what did I do? Did I stay in bed or get out of bed?_____
_____

What did I do in the 1-2 hours before getting into bed?
_____
_____
_____
_____

What did I eat in the 2-3 hours before getting into bed?
_____
_____
_____
_____

Did I nap during the day? Yes / No
If so, for how long?_____

The quality of my sleep last night was:
Poor   1   2   3   4   5   6   7   8   9   10   Excellent

What time did I wake up in the morning? _____

What time did I get out of bed? _____

How rested did I feel in the morning?
Not rested at all   1   2   3   4   5   6   7   8   9   10   Very well rested

Did I have caffeine/nicotine/alcohol during the day? Y/N
What time(s)? _____
_____

What was my level of activity during the day?
Sedentary   Light   Moderate   Active   Extremely Active

Notes:
_____
_____
_____
_____
_____
_____
_____
_____
_____
_____
_____
_____

Day: _____   Date: _____

What time did I get into bed last night? _____

What time did I try to fall sleep? _____

What did I do in the time between getting into bed and trying to
fall sleep? _____

How long did it take me to fall asleep? _____

How many times did I wake during the night? _____

What woke me? (What emotional, physical, environmental or
other factors affected my sleep.)
_____
_____

Was I able to fall back asleep easily? If not, what did I do? Did I
stay in bed or get out of bed?_____
_____

What did I do in the 1-2 hours before getting into bed?
_____
_____
_____
_____

What did I eat in the 2-3 hours before getting into bed?
_____
_____
_____
_____

Did I nap during the day? Yes / No
If so, for how long?_____

The quality of my sleep last night was:
Poor   1   2   3   4   5   6   7   8   9   10   Excellent

What time did I wake up in the morning? _____

What time did I get out of bed? _____

How rested did I feel in the morning?
Not rested at all   1   2   3   4   5   6   7   8   9   10   Very well rested

Did I have caffeine/nicotine/alcohol during the day? Y/N
What time(s)? _____
_____

What was my level of activity during the day?
Sedentary   Light   Moderate   Active   Extremely Active

Notes:
_____
_____
_____
_____
_____
_____
_____
_____
_____
_____
_____
_____

Day: _____ Date: _____

What time did I get into bed last night? _____

What time did I try to fall sleep? _____

What did I do in the time between getting into bed and trying to fall sleep? _____

How long did it take me to fall asleep? _____

How many times did I wake during the night? _____

What woke me? (What emotional, physical, environmental or other factors affected my sleep.)
_____
_____

Was I able to fall back asleep easily? If not, what did I do? Did I stay in bed or get out of bed?_____
_____

What did I do in the 1-2 hours before getting into bed?
_____
_____
_____
_____

What did I eat in the 2-3 hours before getting into bed?
_____
_____
_____
_____

Did I nap during the day? Yes / No
If so, for how long?_____

The quality of my sleep last night was:
Poor   1   2   3   4   5   6   7   8   9   10   Excellent

What time did I wake up in the morning? _____

What time did I get out of bed? _____

How rested did I feel in the morning?
Not rested at all   1   2   3   4   5   6   7   8   9   10   Very well rested

Did I have caffeine/nicotine/alcohol during the day? Y/N
What time(s)? _____
_____

What was my level of activity during the day?
Sedentary   Light   Moderate   Active   Extremely Active

Notes:
_____
_____
_____
_____
_____
_____
_____
_____
_____
_____
_____
_____

Day: _____ Date: _____

What time did I get into bed last night? _____

What time did I try to fall sleep? _____

What did I do in the time between getting into bed and trying to fall sleep? _____

How long did it take me to fall asleep? _____

How many times did I wake during the night? _____

What woke me? (What emotional, physical, environmental or other factors affected my sleep.)
_____
_____

Was I able to fall back asleep easily? If not, what did I do? Did I stay in bed or get out of bed?_____
_____

What did I do in the 1-2 hours before getting into bed?
_____
_____
_____
_____

What did I eat in the 2-3 hours before getting into bed?
_____
_____
_____
_____

Did I nap during the day? Yes / No
If so, for how long?_____

The quality of my sleep last night was:
Poor   1   2   3   4   5   6   7   8   9   10   Excellent

What time did I wake up in the morning? _____

What time did I get out of bed? _____

How rested did I feel in the morning?
Not rested at all   1   2   3   4   5   6   7   8   9   10   Very well rested

Did I have caffeine/nicotine/alcohol during the day? Y/N
What time(s)? _____
_____

What was my level of activity during the day?
Sedentary   Light   Moderate   Active   Extremely Active

Notes:
_____
_____
_____
_____
_____
_____
_____
_____
_____
_____
_____
_____
_____

Day: _____ Date: _____

What time did I get into bed last night? _____

What time did I try to fall sleep? _____

What did I do in the time between getting into bed and trying to fall sleep? _____

How long did it take me to fall asleep? _____

How many times did I wake during the night? _____

What woke me? (What emotional, physical, environmental or other factors affected my sleep.)
_____
_____

Was I able to fall back asleep easily? If not, what did I do? Did I stay in bed or get out of bed?_____
_____

What did I do in the 1-2 hours before getting into bed?
_____
_____
_____
_____

What did I eat in the 2-3 hours before getting into bed?
_____
_____
_____
_____

Did I nap during the day? Yes / No
If so, for how long?_____

The quality of my sleep last night was:
Poor   1   2   3   4   5   6   7   8   9   10   Excellent

What time did I wake up in the morning? _____

What time did I get out of bed? _____

How rested did I feel in the morning?
Not rested at all   1 2 3 4 5 6 7 8 9 10   Very well rested

Did I have caffeine/nicotine/alcohol during the day? Y/N
What time(s)? _____
_____

What was my level of activity during the day?
Sedentary   Light   Moderate   Active   Extremely Active

Notes:
_____
_____
_____
_____
_____
_____
_____
_____
_____
_____
_____
_____

Day: _____ Date: _____

What time did I get into bed last night? _____

What time did I try to fall sleep? _____

What did I do in the time between getting into bed and trying to fall sleep? _____

How long did it take me to fall asleep? _____

How many times did I wake during the night? _____

What woke me? (What emotional, physical, environmental or other factors affected my sleep.)

_____

_____

Was I able to fall back asleep easily? If not, what did I do? Did I stay in bed or get out of bed?_____

_____

What did I do in the 1-2 hours before getting into bed?

_____

_____

_____

_____

What did I eat in the 2-3 hours before getting into bed?

_____

_____

_____

_____

Did I nap during the day? Yes / No
If so, for how long?_____

The quality of my sleep last night was:
Poor   1   2   3   4   5   6   7   8   9   10   Excellent

What time did I wake up in the morning? _____

What time did I get out of bed? _____

How rested did I feel in the morning?
Not rested at all   1   2   3   4   5   6   7   8   9   10   Very well rested

Did I have caffeine/nicotine/alcohol during the day? Y/N
What time(s)? _____
_____

What was my level of activity during the day?
Sedentary   Light   Moderate   Active   Extremely Active

Notes:
_____
_____
_____
_____
_____
_____
_____
_____
_____
_____
_____
_____
_____

Week-at-a-Glance

To track information in a week-at-a-glance, fill in the chart below. This will help you keep track of your basic sleep patterns.

Day of the Week	Day 1	Day 2	Day 3	Day 4	Day 5	Day 6	Day 7
What time did I get into bed?							
What time did I go to sleep?							
Total hours sleep							
Quality of Sleep (1-10)							
What time did I wake up?							
What time did I get out of bed?							
How rested did I feel? (1-10)							

Sleep is that golden chain that ties health and
our bodies together.

--Thomas Dekker

Day: _____ Date: _____

What time did I get into bed last night? _____

What time did I try to fall sleep? _____

What did I do in the time between getting into bed and trying to fall sleep? _____

How long did it take me to fall asleep? _____

How many times did I wake during the night? _____

What woke me? (What emotional, physical, environmental or other factors affected my sleep.)
_____
_____

Was I able to fall back asleep easily? If not, what did I do? Did I stay in bed or get out of bed?_____
_____

What did I do in the 1-2 hours before getting into bed?
_____
_____
_____
_____

What did I eat in the 2-3 hours before getting into bed?
_____
_____
_____
_____

Did I nap during the day? Yes / No
If so, for how long?_____

The quality of my sleep last night was:
Poor   1   2   3   4   5   6   7   8   9   10   Excellent

What time did I wake up in the morning? _____

What time did I get out of bed? _____

How rested did I feel in the morning?
Not rested at all   1   2   3   4   5   6   7   8   9   10   Very well rested

Did I have caffeine/nicotine/alcohol during the day? Y/N
What time(s)? _____
_____

What was my level of activity during the day?
Sedentary   Light   Moderate   Active   Extremely Active

Notes:
_____
_____
_____
_____
_____
_____
_____
_____
_____
_____
_____
_____

Day: _____ Date: _____

What time did I get into bed last night? _____

What time did I try to fall sleep? _____

What did I do in the time between getting into bed and trying to fall sleep? _____

How long did it take me to fall asleep? _____

How many times did I wake during the night? _____

What woke me? (What emotional, physical, environmental or other factors affected my sleep.)

_____

_____

Was I able to fall back asleep easily? If not, what did I do? Did I stay in bed or get out of bed?_____

_____

What did I do in the 1-2 hours before getting into bed?

_____

_____

_____

_____

What did I eat in the 2-3 hours before getting into bed?

_____

_____

_____

_____

Did I nap during the day? Yes / No
If so, for how long?_____

The quality of my sleep last night was:
Poor   1   2   3   4   5   6   7   8   9   10   Excellent

What time did I wake up in the morning? _____

What time did I get out of bed? _____

How rested did I feel in the morning?
Not rested at all   1   2   3   4   5   6   7   8   9   10   Very well rested

Did I have caffeine/nicotine/alcohol during the day? Y/N
What time(s)? _____
_____

What was my level of activity during the day?
Sedentary   Light   Moderate   Active   Extremely Active

Notes:
_____
_____
_____
_____
_____
_____
_____
_____
_____
_____
_____
_____

Day: _____ Date: _____

What time did I get into bed last night? _____

What time did I try to fall sleep? _____

What did I do in the time between getting into bed and trying to fall sleep? _____

How long did it take me to fall asleep? _____

How many times did I wake during the night? _____

What woke me? (What emotional, physical, environmental or other factors affected my sleep.)
_____
_____

Was I able to fall back asleep easily? If not, what did I do? Did I stay in bed or get out of bed?_____
_____

What did I do in the 1-2 hours before getting into bed?
_____
_____
_____
_____

What did I eat in the 2-3 hours before getting into bed?
_____
_____
_____
_____

Did I nap during the day? Yes / No
If so, for how long?_____

The quality of my sleep last night was:
Poor   1   2   3   4   5   6   7   8   9   10   Excellent

What time did I wake up in the morning? _____

What time did I get out of bed? _____

How rested did I feel in the morning?
Not rested at all   1   2   3   4   5   6   7   8   9   10   Very well rested

Did I have caffeine/nicotine/alcohol during the day? Y/N
What time(s)? _____
_____

What was my level of activity during the day?
Sedentary   Light   Moderate   Active   Extremely Active

Notes:
_____
_____
_____
_____
_____
_____
_____
_____
_____
_____
_____
_____

Day: _____ Date: _____

What time did I get into bed last night? _____

What time did I try to fall sleep? _____

What did I do in the time between getting into bed and trying to fall sleep? _____

How long did it take me to fall asleep? _____

How many times did I wake during the night? _____

What woke me? (What emotional, physical, environmental or other factors affected my sleep.)

_____

_____

Was I able to fall back asleep easily? If not, what did I do? Did I stay in bed or get out of bed?_____

_____

What did I do in the 1-2 hours before getting into bed?

_____

_____

_____

_____

What did I eat in the 2-3 hours before getting into bed?

_____

_____

_____

_____

Did I nap during the day? Yes / No
If so, for how long?_____

The quality of my sleep last night was:
Poor   1   2   3   4   5   6   7   8   9   10   Excellent

What time did I wake up in the morning? _____

What time did I get out of bed? _____

How rested did I feel in the morning?
Not rested at all   1   2   3   4   5   6   7   8   9   10   Very well rested

Did I have caffeine/nicotine/alcohol during the day? Y/N
What time(s)? _____
_____

What was my level of activity during the day?
Sedentary   Light   Moderate   Active   Extremely Active

Notes:
_____
_____
_____
_____
_____
_____
_____
_____
_____
_____
_____
_____

Day: _____ Date: _____

What time did I get into bed last night? _____

What time did I try to fall sleep? _____

What did I do in the time between getting into bed and trying to
fall sleep? _____

How long did it take me to fall asleep? _____

How many times did I wake during the night? _____

What woke me? (What emotional, physical, environmental or
other factors affected my sleep.)

_____
_____

Was I able to fall back asleep easily? If not, what did I do? Did I
stay in bed or get out of bed?_____
_____

What did I do in the 1-2 hours before getting into bed?

_____
_____
_____
_____

What did I eat in the 2-3 hours before getting into bed?

_____
_____
_____
_____

Did I nap during the day? Yes / No
If so, for how long?_____

The quality of my sleep last night was:
Poor   1   2   3   4   5   6   7   8   9   10   Excellent

What time did I wake up in the morning? _____

What time did I get out of bed? _____

How rested did I feel in the morning?
Not rested at all   1   2   3   4   5   6   7   8   9   10   Very well rested

Did I have caffeine/nicotine/alcohol during the day? Y/N
What time(s)? _____
_____

What was my level of activity during the day?
Sedentary   Light   Moderate   Active   Extremely Active

Notes:
_____
_____
_____
_____
_____
_____
_____
_____
_____
_____
_____
_____
_____

Day: _____   Date: _____

What time did I get into bed last night? _____

What time did I try to fall sleep? _____

What did I do in the time between getting into bed and trying to fall sleep? _____

How long did it take me to fall asleep? _____

How many times did I wake during the night? _____

What woke me? (What emotional, physical, environmental or other factors affected my sleep.)
_____
_____

Was I able to fall back asleep easily? If not, what did I do? Did I stay in bed or get out of bed?_____
_____

What did I do in the 1-2 hours before getting into bed?
_____
_____
_____
_____

What did I eat in the 2-3 hours before getting into bed?
_____
_____
_____
_____

Did I nap during the day? Yes / No
If so, for how long?_____

The quality of my sleep last night was:
Poor   1   2   3   4   5   6   7   8   9   10   Excellent

What time did I wake up in the morning? _____

What time did I get out of bed? _____

How rested did I feel in the morning?
Not rested at all   1   2   3   4   5   6   7   8   9   10   Very well rested

Did I have caffeine/nicotine/alcohol during the day? Y/N
What time(s)? _____
_____

What was my level of activity during the day?
Sedentary   Light   Moderate   Active   Extremely Active

Notes:
_____
_____
_____
_____
_____
_____
_____
_____
_____
_____
_____
_____

Day: _____ Date: _____

What time did I get into bed last night? _____

What time did I try to fall sleep? _____

What did I do in the time between getting into bed and trying to fall sleep? _____

How long did it take me to fall asleep? _____

How many times did I wake during the night? _____

What woke me? (What emotional, physical, environmental or other factors affected my sleep.)
_____
_____

Was I able to fall back asleep easily? If not, what did I do? Did I stay in bed or get out of bed?_____
_____

What did I do in the 1-2 hours before getting into bed?
_____
_____
_____
_____

What did I eat in the 2-3 hours before getting into bed?
_____
_____
_____
_____

Did I nap during the day? Yes / No
If so, for how long?_____

The quality of my sleep last night was:
Poor   1   2   3   4   5   6   7   8   9   10   Excellent

What time did I wake up in the morning? _____

What time did I get out of bed? _____

How rested did I feel in the morning?
Not rested at all   1   2   3   4   5   6   7   8   9   10   Very well rested

Did I have caffeine/nicotine/alcohol during the day? Y/N
What time(s)? _____
_____

What was my level of activity during the day?
Sedentary   Light   Moderate   Active   Extremely Active

Notes:
_____
_____
_____
_____
_____
_____
_____
_____
_____
_____
_____
_____

Week-at-a-Glance

To track information in a week-at-a-glance, fill in the chart below. This will help you keep track of your basic sleep patterns.

Day of the Week	Day 1	Day 2	Day 3	Day 4	Day 5	Day 6	Day 7
What time did I get into bed?							
What time did I go to sleep?							
Total hours sleep							
Quality of Sleep (1-10)							
What time did I wake up?							
What time did I get out of bed?							
How rested did I feel? (1-10)							

Sleep is an under-ocean dipped into each night.

--Jim Morrison

Day: _____   Date: _____

What time did I get into bed last night? _____

What time did I try to fall sleep? _____

What did I do in the time between getting into bed and trying to fall sleep? _____

How long did it take me to fall asleep? _____

How many times did I wake during the night? _____

What woke me? (What emotional, physical, environmental or other factors affected my sleep.)

_____

_____

Was I able to fall back asleep easily? If not, what did I do? Did I stay in bed or get out of bed?_____

_____

What did I do in the 1-2 hours before getting into bed?

_____

_____

_____

_____

What did I eat in the 2-3 hours before getting into bed?

_____

_____

_____

_____

Did I nap during the day? Yes / No
If so, for how long?_____

The quality of my sleep last night was:
Poor   1   2   3   4   5   6   7   8   9   10   Excellent

What time did I wake up in the morning? _____

What time did I get out of bed? _____

How rested did I feel in the morning?
Not rested at all   1   2   3   4   5   6   7   8   9   10   Very well rested

Did I have caffeine/nicotine/alcohol during the day? Y/N
What time(s)? _____
_____

What was my level of activity during the day?
Sedentary   Light   Moderate   Active   Extremely Active

Notes:
_____
_____
_____
_____
_____
_____
_____
_____
_____
_____
_____
_____

Day: _____ Date: _____

What time did I get into bed last night? _____

What time did I try to fall sleep? _____

What did I do in the time between getting into bed and trying to fall sleep? _____

How long did it take me to fall asleep? _____

How many times did I wake during the night? _____

What woke me? (What emotional, physical, environmental or other factors affected my sleep.)

_____

_____

Was I able to fall back asleep easily? If not, what did I do? Did I stay in bed or get out of bed?_____

_____

What did I do in the 1-2 hours before getting into bed?

_____

_____

_____

_____

What did I eat in the 2-3 hours before getting into bed?

_____

_____

_____

_____

Did I nap during the day? Yes / No
If so, for how long?_____

The quality of my sleep last night was:
Poor   1   2   3   4   5   6   7   8   9   10   Excellent

What time did I wake up in the morning? _____

What time did I get out of bed? _____

How rested did I feel in the morning?
Not rested at all   1   2   3   4   5   6   7   8   9   10   Very well rested

Did I have caffeine/nicotine/alcohol during the day? Y/N
What time(s)? _____
_____

What was my level of activity during the day?
Sedentary   Light   Moderate   Active   Extremely Active

Notes:
_____
_____
_____
_____
_____
_____
_____
_____
_____
_____
_____
_____

Day: _____ Date: _____

What time did I get into bed last night? _____

What time did I try to fall sleep? _____

What did I do in the time between getting into bed and trying to fall sleep? _____

How long did it take me to fall asleep? _____

How many times did I wake during the night? _____

What woke me? (What emotional, physical, environmental or other factors affected my sleep.)

_____

_____

Was I able to fall back asleep easily? If not, what did I do? Did I stay in bed or get out of bed?_____

_____

What did I do in the 1-2 hours before getting into bed?

_____

_____

_____

_____

What did I eat in the 2-3 hours before getting into bed?

_____

_____

_____

_____

Did I nap during the day? Yes / No
If so, for how long?_____

The quality of my sleep last night was:
Poor   1   2   3   4   5   6   7   8   9   10   Excellent

What time did I wake up in the morning? _____

What time did I get out of bed? _____

How rested did I feel in the morning?
Not rested at all   1   2   3   4   5   6   7   8   9   10   Very well rested

Did I have caffeine/nicotine/alcohol during the day? Y/N
What time(s)? _____
_____

What was my level of activity during the day?
Sedentary   Light   Moderate   Active   Extremely Active

Notes:
_____
_____
_____
_____
_____
_____
_____
_____
_____
_____
_____
_____

Day: _____ Date: _____

What time did I get into bed last night? _____

What time did I try to fall sleep? _____

What did I do in the time between getting into bed and trying to fall sleep? _____

How long did it take me to fall asleep? _____

How many times did I wake during the night? _____

What woke me? (What emotional, physical, environmental or other factors affected my sleep.)

_____

_____

Was I able to fall back asleep easily? If not, what did I do? Did I stay in bed or get out of bed? _____

_____

What did I do in the 1-2 hours before getting into bed?

_____

_____

_____

_____

What did I eat in the 2-3 hours before getting into bed?

_____

_____

_____

_____

Did I nap during the day? Yes / No
If so, for how long?_____

The quality of my sleep last night was:
Poor   1   2   3   4   5   6   7   8   9   10   Excellent

What time did I wake up in the morning? _____

What time did I get out of bed? _____

How rested did I feel in the morning?
Not rested at all   1   2   3   4   5   6   7   8   9   10   Very well rested

Did I have caffeine/nicotine/alcohol during the day? Y/N
What time(s)? _____
_____

What was my level of activity during the day?
Sedentary   Light   Moderate   Active   Extremely Active

Notes:
_____
_____
_____
_____
_____
_____
_____
_____
_____
_____
_____
_____
_____

Day: _____ Date: _____

What time did I get into bed last night? _____

What time did I try to fall sleep? _____

What did I do in the time between getting into bed and trying to fall sleep? _____

How long did it take me to fall asleep? _____

How many times did I wake during the night? _____

What woke me? (What emotional, physical, environmental or other factors affected my sleep.)
_____
_____

Was I able to fall back asleep easily? If not, what did I do? Did I stay in bed or get out of bed?_____
_____

What did I do in the 1-2 hours before getting into bed?
_____
_____
_____
_____

What did I eat in the 2-3 hours before getting into bed?
_____
_____
_____
_____

Did I nap during the day? Yes / No
If so, for how long?_____

The quality of my sleep last night was:
Poor   1   2   3   4   5   6   7   8   9   10   Excellent

What time did I wake up in the morning? _____

What time did I get out of bed? _____

How rested did I feel in the morning?
Not rested at all   1   2   3   4   5   6   7   8   9   10   Very well rested

Did I have caffeine/nicotine/alcohol during the day? Y/N
What time(s)? _____
_____

What was my level of activity during the day?
Sedentary   Light   Moderate   Active   Extremely Active

Notes:
_____
_____
_____
_____
_____
_____
_____
_____
_____
_____
_____
_____

Day: _____ Date: _____

What time did I get into bed last night? _____

What time did I try to fall sleep? _____

What did I do in the time between getting into bed and trying to fall sleep? _____

How long did it take me to fall asleep? _____

How many times did I wake during the night? _____

What woke me? (What emotional, physical, environmental or other factors affected my sleep.)

_____

_____

Was I able to fall back asleep easily? If not, what did I do? Did I stay in bed or get out of bed?_____

_____

What did I do in the 1-2 hours before getting into bed?

_____

_____

_____

_____

What did I eat in the 2-3 hours before getting into bed?

_____

_____

_____

_____

Did I nap during the day? Yes / No
If so, for how long?_____

The quality of my sleep last night was:
Poor   1   2   3   4   5   6   7   8   9   10   Excellent

What time did I wake up in the morning? _____

What time did I get out of bed? _____

How rested did I feel in the morning?
Not rested at all   1   2   3   4   5   6   7   8   9   10   Very well rested

Did I have caffeine/nicotine/alcohol during the day? Y/N
What time(s)? _____
_____

What was my level of activity during the day?
Sedentary   Light   Moderate   Active   Extremely Active

Notes:
_____
_____
_____
_____
_____
_____
_____
_____
_____
_____
_____
_____
_____

Day: _____ Date: _____

What time did I get into bed last night? _____

What time did I try to fall sleep? _____

What did I do in the time between getting into bed and trying to fall sleep? _____

How long did it take me to fall asleep? _____

How many times did I wake during the night? _____

What woke me? (What emotional, physical, environmental or other factors affected my sleep.)
_____
_____

Was I able to fall back asleep easily? If not, what did I do? Did I stay in bed or get out of bed?_____
_____

What did I do in the 1-2 hours before getting into bed?
_____
_____
_____
_____

What did I eat in the 2-3 hours before getting into bed?
_____
_____
_____
_____

Did I nap during the day? Yes / No
If so, for how long?_____

The quality of my sleep last night was:
Poor   1   2   3   4   5   6   7   8   9   10   Excellent

What time did I wake up in the morning? _____

What time did I get out of bed? _____

How rested did I feel in the morning?
Not rested at all   1   2   3   4   5   6   7   8   9   10   Very well rested

Did I have caffeine/nicotine/alcohol during the day? Y/N
What time(s)? _____
_____

What was my level of activity during the day?
Sedentary   Light   Moderate   Active   Extremely Active

Notes:
_____
_____
_____
_____
_____
_____
_____
_____
_____
_____
_____
_____

Week-at-a-Glance

To track information in a week-at-a-glance, fill in the chart below. This will help you keep track of your basic sleep patterns.

Day of the Week	Day 1	Day 2	Day 3	Day 4	Day 5	Day 6	Day 7
What time did I get into bed?							
What time did I go to sleep?							
Total hours sleep							
Quality of Sleep (1-10)							
What time did I wake up?							
What time did I get out of bed?							
How rested did I feel? (1-10)							

Trust in dreams, for in them is hidden the gate to eternity.

--Kahlil Gibran

DREAMS

Date: _____ Dream: _____

Date: _____ Dream: _____

_____
_____
_____
_____
_____
_____
_____
_____
_____
_____
_____
_____
_____
_____
_____
_____
_____
_____
_____
_____
_____
_____
_____
_____
_____
_____
_____
_____
_____
_____
_____
_____

Date: _____   Dream: _____

_____
_____
_____
_____
_____
_____
_____
_____
_____
_____
_____
_____
_____
_____
_____
_____
_____
_____
_____
_____
_____
_____
_____
_____
_____
_____
_____
_____
_____
_____
_____
_____
_____
_____

Date: _____ Dream: _____

_____
_____
_____
_____
_____
_____
_____
_____
_____
_____
_____
_____
_____
_____
_____
_____
_____
_____
_____
_____
_____
_____
_____
_____
_____
_____
_____
_____
_____

Date: _____   Dream: _____

_____
_____
_____
_____
_____
_____
_____
_____
_____
_____
_____
_____
_____
_____
_____
_____
_____
_____
_____
_____
_____
_____
_____
_____
_____
_____
_____
_____
_____
_____

Date: _____   Dream: _____

Date: _____   Dream: _____

_____
_____
_____
_____
_____
_____
_____
_____
_____
_____
_____
_____
_____
_____
_____
_____
_____
_____
_____
_____
_____
_____
_____
_____
_____
_____
_____
_____
_____

Date: _____ Dream: _____

_____
_____
_____
_____
_____
_____
_____
_____
_____
_____
_____
_____
_____
_____
_____
_____
_____
_____
_____
_____
_____
_____
_____
_____
_____
_____
_____
_____
_____
_____
_____
_____

Date: _____ Dream: _____

_____
_____
_____
_____
_____
_____
_____
_____
_____
_____
_____
_____
_____
_____
_____
_____
_____
_____
_____
_____
_____
_____
_____
_____
_____
_____
_____
_____
_____
_____
_____

Date: _____   Dream: _____

_____
_____
_____
_____
_____
_____
_____
_____
_____
_____
_____
_____
_____
_____
_____
_____
_____
_____
_____
_____
_____
_____
_____
_____
_____

Date: _____ Dream: _____

_____
_____
_____
_____
_____
_____
_____
_____
_____
_____
_____
_____
_____
_____
_____
_____
_____
_____
_____
_____
_____
_____
_____
_____
_____
_____
_____
_____
_____
_____
_____
_____

Date: _____ Dream: _____

_____
_____
_____
_____
_____
_____
_____
_____
_____
_____
_____
_____
_____
_____
_____
_____
_____
_____
_____
_____
_____
_____
_____
_____
_____
_____
_____
_____
_____

Other Guided Journals by Premise Content:

Dream Journal

Prayer Journal

Gratitude Journal

Recipe Journal

Eating Awareness for Emotional Eaters

Eating Awareness for Binge Eaters

Daily Food Journal

Food & Feelings Journal

Personal Food and Health Tracker

To see other Premise Content journals in a wide variety of
covers and interiors, visit our page on Amazon at
amazon.com/author/premisecontent

or

visit our website at www.premisecontent.com.

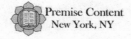
Premise Content
New York, NY

Made in the USA
Monee, IL
25 January 2021

58609780R10090